IMPRESSIONS

Thomas Joyce

authorHOUSE®

AuthorHouse™
1663 Liberty Drive
Bloomington, IN 47403
www.authorhouse.com
Phone: 1-800-839-8640

First published by AuthorHouse 4/29/2009

ISBN: 978-1-4389-8323-3 (sc)

Printed in the United States of America
Bloomington, Indiana

This book is printed on acid-free paper.

1.

I dreamt of
you
and distance
as I so very often
do
and your words
filled the air with
red rose
petals
like Saint Theresa's
vow

2.

Our house is
a forest
its' turrets like
branches
grey as doves
against a greyer
moon
but within
we spin epics
lit by storms
and candles all
watched
by our
 Buddha
of bottomless eyes

3.

She drifts
upon the nights one
into another till
life itself
becomes but
a gospel of
wondrous one-act
passions
weeping
raging at the stars
then
languid dreamy
homespun
I cloak myself in
triumph
and pass
among her
blessings

4.

the comforts of
most men are
alien to me
I lack fulfillment
here
in my torso
I wish for something
anything
other than
these
great Gaelic
wings
and their
manic ceaseless
thunder

5.

man is but a
divine beast
caged sometimes
not
claiming all
then
blind, withered
cancer-stricken

undone

I lie in bed
through the thickening nights
the soft high
song of the grass
fills me
waiting
waiting

6.

all along
the bay
the summer willows
stand
their branches
 flow
as pale
thin waves
on a vast
clear ocean
of light

7.

at this point
I am so far away
from nothingness
up to my eyelids
in passions
awash in this blossoming
miracle
 I have somehow
fell upon
at this point when
self and ego
fade like
dappled sunlight on
the timeless blue
Niagara
here I cast my lot
upon my bones; my steps
upon my feet

8.

My life is as
a web of stars
ancient
in their sorrows
naked
roaming
orbs of fate
suns and hearts
and eyes

9.

face up
and the sun
like an enormous
orange
Buddha
squats on
my chest
stares down
on me
with a child's
wonder
whispers one
word
and then smiles

10.

walk abroad
these tea-green
gardens
resplendent in
your summer
things and I
will set
my place
beside you
and stay to
hear
your robins
sing

11.

I drank rage
 daily;
made Zen moments
rare
made Franciscan imaginings
seem like
continents
away
but
 now and again
I ate peace
digesting Gandhi
 and the Buddha
like
chocolates

12.

Do yellow Russian
flowers grow
on Dostoevsky's grave?
I wouldn't know
about that
but I have
stood among the rains
at Yeats' rocky bed
and found him
dreaming
(through the stones)
of centaurs
on the beach

13.

my love is
solitary
coveted
wrapped in sheets
of being
she waits and sits
like potted
seed;
how joyous is
her blooming

14.

composing poems
in the bath
imagining pyramids
growing under my
street
I hear them straining
through cancerous roots and
pipes of hermetic
suburban repression
to burst forth
like flowers and
angels of empathy
streaming perfect sunshine
all through the
windows next
door
where I hear
St. Augustine
playing his drum
while Bukowski
blows sax and
Lermontov fiddles

15.

Now you tell me Kaufman
didn't breath for 10 years
and Snyder became
unto
an ivory smooth Buddha
while McClure
woke up
one day
to be that joyful
brass trumpet
he'd been secretly polishing
all those
long years
in the
end- of -land
night

16.

painted
golden scriptures
on sails of azure flame
set forth on cloud dimmed
merchant seas
like sacred locusts
or winged beetle-monks
as bare-chested souls
(small and fragile)
squat on the beach their
hands in the sand
singing the
hymns of
the turtle

17.

kiss me goodbye
in the morning
in the blush-rose
hour your face
China white
smoothly polished
as pebbles
arrayed at
our feet
grasp me with your
bent Lotus eyes
cast me to streams
of one-ness
on currents
that glide
through your
tangerine groves

18.

Sentimental village
girls lost in
winds and rains and
leaves each year
this season calls
them back to stand
in raptured
aching
silence
"could have beens"
whirl through
half forgotten
streets and parks
so grey and yellow
while Northeastern
waltzes fill the air and
long dead
apron draped mothers
beckon from porches
and stairs climb
to nothingness
dark as an
Indian princess
who sleeps with
the trees
and the ghosts
and the secrets
she keeps with
the ferns
by the Iroquois sea

19.

Rimbaud
drunk as hell
on the bright pagan
veldt
crotch deep in
sins and ivory
how far from
slums and lice
and madness
swirling in rank
English gutters
we live on a
cancer;
a verdant green
tumor
a pox on
Vishnu's' blue
face

20.

I have quit the Jason Quest
fair one;
the truth you may take
to your dark bed
to be spoken of
only by crows

21.

I had flowers
once
of little white bones and
grassy thin hair
tiny pitter-patter
hearts like
match head flames
I cupped in
the wild breezes
and then
gone to smoke
and torn crepes
the house
grew big then
and indelicate little
frails
took their spaces
and drove me
under where
I soaked
for a time
till your hand
broke the surface
and dragged me
sputtering
to the Zen colored
sands

22.

why have you turned your
back to me?
I walked through the streets
of Manhattan with you
and drank of your
homemade wine
I slept in your
embrace
and dreamt upon
your pillow
I played your saxophone
to the stars
and never thought
of leavin

23.

leaves today
that I watched going
spinning in circles
climbing the wind
and filling our air
with goodbyes

leaves today
sped past your door;
I dreamt I was among them

24.

gathering chestnuts purely
for the shine
snowflakes were crystal
dervishes in the winking
yellow streetlight
we would climb the
Finest Trees
and race our sacred paths
when the days were so long
and the nights
ran like thieves

25.

2 of us
lost moments past
far from anything
we could
call a home
choosing instead to
inhabit the earth
and splash about in
her lakes

26.

Trafalgar square
in April old
soldiers nodding lightly
their heads are filled
with war
dreams and they float
like
tethered zeppelins

27.

sunflowers crown
her garden
the tree is thick with
bluebirds I wish
I shared those
hours pressed
within her open
glass
sleep must be Elysian there
each fluttered lash
a promise

28.

the fireflies I
chased as a boy
burned brighter far
still today
than the glowingest engines
of industry

29.

so many hawks
Virginia mornings
smiles left behind
my young stranger
running away
her brown eyes telling this
old heart fables

30.

where is there
left to go when
you have known love?
No fireworks over
Hong Kong harbor
(even in the year of the dragon)
could light my eyes with
inspiration
as your easy smile or
one hair left on
my shoulder

31.

Walt Whitman
aloft on silver
smooth wings
effortlessly gliding
down and around
yellow Appalachian
footpaths
as filled with the
sorrows of
cosmic divorce as
that little bare
Indian girl
brown in the sand

32.

Sunday clouds bring
memories
of soulful lightning ballads
and blues in the
toll of raindrops
you're still home
I know you are
but where do you
think I am?
far away
yes
but not so far that
I can't hear the soft song
of your breathing
or smell you even
in the mist of
orange blossoms

33.

cant sing
cant
sing;
no arias rush
from my
spectral depths
cant feel
feel again
your original
promise
kept cold
what a prison
I have turned out
to be

34.

blues like
country dusk
cotton field baseball
sing out in your
shirtless October
cornfields
whisper
and praise that
cricket moon
filling your ears
friends
like tigers
awake in the grass

35.

saying goodbye
with the morning
and the moon still
and soft
on the hills
I have come far
from laying beside you
to this life out
among the winds

36.

Standing on the precipice
of countless epic mornings
high above the winds and foam
a sea of faces
stretches infinite
each one wet and ruined
with the look of
 your goodbye

37.

2 ducks in winged race
I saw cleaving the
salmon-hued skies in
the last moaning days
of winters passing and
as the winds painted ebon waves
across the flowing ices I heard
from low within those depths
Gaea's unanswered sobbing
"Do my young ask me
to dry their tears or
just count them
in their falling"?

38.

so this is the lone path left to us
find a penitent innocent and blameless
 with a soul golden as sheaves of barley in the late
autumn sun
and cast upon
his thrice-cursed shoulders
our blinding raging ignorance. wars
and hungers visited, age by age, from man to
other.
a pitiless wheel spins its sins
cycles and rises
age by age
man to other.

yet sages mark well
this lesson unlearned
 (which itself is the root of our rotting)
such a one such a gate has been through and yes
left open
unthreatened, to be true, in the face of our pride
and the grim stench of
our loathing's;
blessed were we by the arm of a tree
such madness that we choose forgetting.

39.

surfs up
years grown long
blue pirate skies
now weathered and creased
like a paper cup skippin'
the highway
surfsup indeed
for comrades and foes
and old waterways
and gone mama gone
drenched from the spray
from that promise
let others wilt
having never flowered
it's no different but
you and me we stay
as wet as we please
like the streets summer
mornings in Paris
surfs up?
how far from home?
from the true love
that keeps passing through?
these paintings and poems
they live here inside now
and there
in the midst of your wonder
call it what you will
but it's all waves just the same
surfs up and I'm primed
for ridin

40.

lucky are they who
live when they are
not in melancholia stupors
for days one never
knew gleamed only from
paper and nitrate and
I know Central City is
lost/neverwas but
much of it did and
was done and oh how
much better it seemed
with those billowing clouds
and dresses and that long-gone
ball park when it
breathed in the sun

41.

one day I'll
paint a rhapsody
culled from sweetest
memory
and each drop of word
each stroke of light
will stem from your
wan smile

42.

this one
this wanton child
of vulgar Dionysian
passions
weighed down by
the other
like Baudelaire's
chimera;
in all his myriad
appearances and
all his roar
and plodding
he pulls
at me he
drowns my
self in
this lake I've found
inside

43.

Hail to thee
to thee gone
to thee
just 29 and now
of the waves
to thee triumphant
in thy
fleeting
soaring
splendor
hail to thee
adrift in
quiet depths
hail to thee
freed of sorrow
hail to thee
in thy singing green
tomb
where rippled
echoes
play
in time to
thy eternal
verse

44.

drowsy shepherds
stretching limbs
in blooming
life pastoral
wine-stained naked
in sea-blue grasses
far from the road
from din and from
thunder far from
 maidens
with gypsy dark mouths
every day dying
every day
knowing and weeping

45.

winter fell
and sits upon us
settling deep
in hunger scarred valleys
in the pine scented
clans (whose bones are the hills)
who keen all
 the woeful days
whence came the binds
that hold them
to such pitiless hollows
 as those?
They say it's the face of God
which they find
in the clear splashing brooks
by their hovels
but *I* think its
the song of small
voices that rise
from the flowery graves
of their children

46.

the impression you
made on us
as a child was all
impish smiles and
crazy blonde
movement such
primal memories long
the stuff of gathered
legends
and then
and then
other attractions
more immediate desires
more quietly desperate than
ever dreamed in early
snowfall wanderings
came to hold sway

for both of us but
you
never came back you
became further gone
you stayed there
in place you
rusted and failed
now gone,
as you are,
another cog of
those spinning
days lost
(and the rest of them going)
fewer now the
faces and half recalled
wonders yet
I see them still as
the wind-driven clouds
bring me to when
we were we

47.

She carries
ragged red
prairies on
her peasant-thin
shoulders her
neck like a sapling
sunburned and
proud
we fall like the snow
like locusts
like Adam
we campaign
in the hills
bodies sweet
from the
grass

48.

All opened up
to the neon
hot nights
making my
way I feel
God's perfect
jazz feel His head nodding
all around
among the
rooftops and
antennas feel
his breath
on my face
wet and flushed
from tears
hear Him hum
in the subways
all the way
out to the
lake and the
days since
forgotten
sublime in
their going
God's hand
at my window
shy
fingers of light

49.

I see your
face each time
I open my
umbrella
it shines
back at me
even from the
polished stone
of the brown skin
girl's new
necklace

50.

clear Palomino skies
in the vast ruins
of her leaving
the shrouded dry
plains that
hold out their
red arms and call
bare and wild
to the desolate winds

51.

1,000 cranes flew
past my door
with wings of mythic lace
they search across the
mirrored hills
for god's reflected grace

1,000 cranes with
rainbow necks
and eyes of opal night
that cut within the
cloud-deep skies
like arrows white on white

52.

Time in Lowell
slow and hilly
steep streets
windy brick
canal side and
black water
dream pipes
Oklahoma sad
girl sharing her bed
in the tree dark
slowness of passing
three color eyes
mattress on floor
warm as any
he's fell in

53.

Sing to me
of railroads
and dreams born
of iron and coal
share with me
hymns of the
byways and
legends that
lie untold

hold me through
prairies of sorrow
color your sunset
with mine
show me your beaches
of memory
to wade in the
ribbons of time

drink with me
spirits of wonder
grasp forests of stars
in your hands
for we are the
children of summer
and you are the
soul of the land

54.

Dreamin bout
the Spanish steps
and silk scarves
like rainbows
in the fingers
of maidens
I pass silent
through brush stroke
Renaissance twilight
where fawn limbed
virgins in
oil paint bloom
float in delicate
majesty above the
Latin ruins

55.

This wheel it sits
in the back of a shed
in a yard on a street
in a town blue with dying
where green grass grows
yellow grows damp as the
graves of the old men
in autumn
this wheel which once
rolled free as Paradise
down pavements and roads
and trespassed again and
again through that
unknowable country and
then
just like that
it grew pale from the
spinning and changed
to a fossil;
wondrous in it's lack
of motion

56.

I wish America
were a wave
sepia-toned long board land
of sleep-in sun brown skin
and lazy drunk twilights
and walls without clocks
and what we need more of
around here
these days
are wet bathing suits and
sand on the dashboard

57.

I was reminded
that I dreamt
of wrens and
bare summer skin
and your 3 A.M. smile
and trails
we'll one day
stream along
unwinding hearts
like ribbons

silver in the
silver sky

58.

he was an
immigrant
black as rain
she was the
eyes of Allah
his bird sang to
the emerald dawn
brought in the
wake
of her
of passing

59.

I know restaurant
window happenings
counter top
infatuations
born over
gravy and meatloaf and
movies with
endings obscured
by hair-tangled
love making

60.

I read of your
trip in longhand
postcards
dropped by passing
seaplanes
that spread your
words like
yellow wings
upon the
sun-splashed cliffs

61.

I can still see
that brave steeple
rising high in
the dark summer
thunder;
oh how the moon
crested when
I was still a child

62.

Epitaphs written
in sand and trees
dipping their
palms in the
warm Sea of Youth
cloistered in the
silver mines
hidden in the
Byron fields
we rode the tracks
where lanterns
wave
to catch the
rains' slow
progress

63.

Thinkin bout
thrashers headin
out with the mornings
and the fact that I'm
dying
thinkin bout
cold hard mornings
and "I'm goin"
tears fresh
on her pillow
and stars falling clear
in the mountains
and brown eyes

and brown eyes

64.

Soon it'll be
the black ice nightscape
here and all
down to the
Allegany Mountain
ancient place a
tea cup lake
just fit for a giant
and I will trap
for us
owl – eyed in
the hyacinth fields
and share bread
with you in
the morning low
gauze
naked under
gifts of bear

65.

I ran
Saturday
Summer Sundays
post-thin legs
tireless
bounding
burning
rail tracks
rotting and
rolling
around us
the moon
was an apple
ripe
brilliant
departing

66.

There were boys
who once grew
in the glow of
perpetual small town
summer vacation
run-about
blinding bliss
of swimming pool
chlorine kingdoms
who snow-ball
fought
roof top
sneakers climbed
trees
named their conquests
through leaves
velvet green
then rolled
in their redness
October
laughed all
Christmas long
had dogs
wagging loyal
and sisters
"shy in the doorway"
in the joyous
dew morning on

their strange
winding
stairs
had mothers
iron smoothed
always at
home
those boys
grew to men
who ended up
in a bottle
crawled
right inside
tugged the cap

tight
behind them
and sisters
and mothers
and dogs
all of those
measures of fame
in the empire
of time
went to amber
one stone from
forgotten

67.

All of us together
(as if in unity those tigers
could be kept at bay...
even caged)
we grasped at each other
and all others
with green hands
glanced at each other
never stared
with eyes white with glass
and tried as the unrequited have
struggled for epochs
to see to touch to find console
and solace to curl up
like a link shiny confident proud
chain me
chain us
confine me for sure
imprison us always
(to the last son and daughter)
inside that collective
we never achieved

68.

The cool bones
of parting
left there
on a porch
the curve of
 a shoulder
cut smooth from
the dawn
and yet her
morning
suntan lines
sit traced upon
my dreams

69.

I know trains
and the songs
of their passing
they echo with
flight through this
homeland
of dreams
I know the sounds
of light footsteps
descending
and the anguish
of calico
brushing the doorway

Printed in the United States
217251BV00001B/2/P

9 781438 983233